Chemical Reactions

by Daniel R. Faust

Consultant: Sara Vogt
Science Educator at Anoka Hennepin School District

BEARPORT
PUBLISHING

Minneapolis, Minnesota

Credits

Cover and title page, © MichalLudwiczak/iStock; 5, © Chris Ryan/iStock; 9, © Sansanorth/Shutterstock; 11, © d1sk/Shutterstock; 12–13, © kidkatster/Shutterstock; 19, © MEE KO DONG/Shutterstock; 21, © Lukas Gojda/Shutterstock; 23T, © TFoxFoto/Shutterstock; 23B, © kasarp studio/Shutterstock; 25, © antoniodiaz/Shutterstock; and 27, © Sinichenko Maksim/Shutterstock.

Bearport Publishing Company Product Development Team

President: Jen Jenson; Director of Product Development: Spencer Brinker; Senior Editor: Allison Juda; Editor: Charly Haley; Associate Editor: Naomi Reich; Senior Designer: Colin O'Dea; Associate Designer: Elena Klinkner; Associate Designer: Kayla Eggert; Product Development Assistant: Anita Stasson

Library of Congress Cataloging-in-Publication Data

Names: Faust, Daniel R., author.
Title: Chemical reactions / by Daniel R. Faust.
Description: Minneapolis, Minnesota : Bearport Publishing Company, [2023] | Series: Intro to chemistry: need to know | Includes bibliographical references and index.
Identifiers: LCCN 2022033636 (print) | LCCN 2022033637 (ebook) | ISBN 9798885094245 (library binding) | ISBN 9798885095464 (paperback) | ISBN 9798885096614 (ebook)
Subjects: LCSH: Chemical reactions—Juvenile literature. | Chemistry—Juvenile literature.
Classification: LCC QD501 .F2985 2023 (print) | LCC QD501 (ebook) | DDC 541/.39—dc23/eng/20220719
LC record available at https://lccn.loc.gov/2022033636
LC ebook record available at https://lccn.loc.gov/2022033637

For more information, write to Bearport Publishing, 5357 Penn Avenue South, Minneapolis, MN 55419.

Contents

Make a Wish

Candles flicker on your birthday cake. With a quick blow, you put them out. Time to celebrate!

But what makes the candles burn in the first place? Why do the flames go out with a puff of air? It's all thanks to chemical reactions.

What do you see after you blow out a candle? Smoke curls up from where the flame used to be. Another chemical reaction has happened.

Bound to Be

How do reactions happen? It has to do with the smallest parts of our universe. Everything is made of matter. And matter is made of tiny **atoms**. Each atom has even smaller parts. They are called protons, neutrons, and electrons.

Protons and neutrons are at the middle of each atom. Electrons move around the middle. Different kinds of atoms have different numbers of protons, neutrons, and electrons.

A Model of an Atom

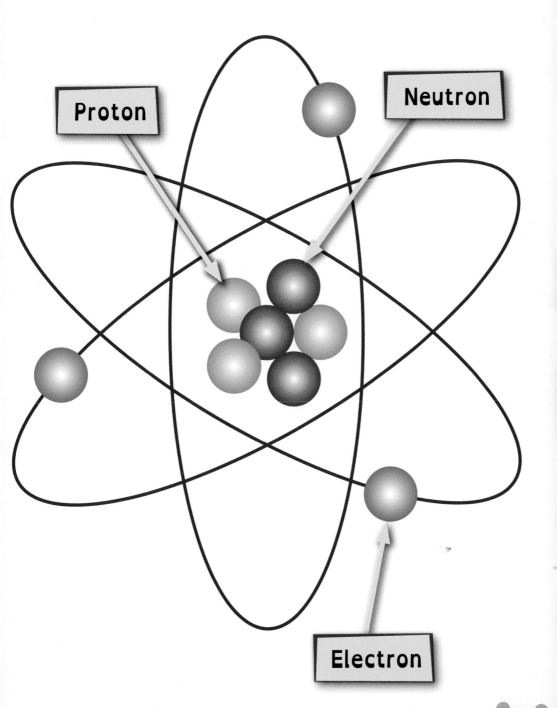

Two or more atoms can come together to form **molecules**. How? Sometimes, an atom is missing an electron. To get to its full number, it may share an electron with another atom. This joins the atoms through a chemical bond. It keeps molecules together.

Chemical bonds always form in pairs of electrons. Atoms may have bonds with just one pair of electrons. It can also happen with two or three pairs.

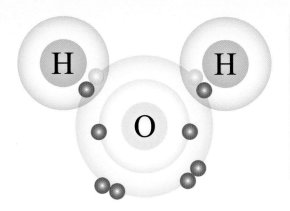

Molecules need at least one set of bonded electrons. This one has two single bonds.

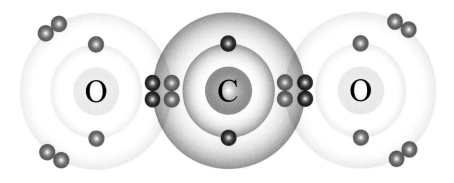

This molecule has two bonded pairs connecting each set of atoms.

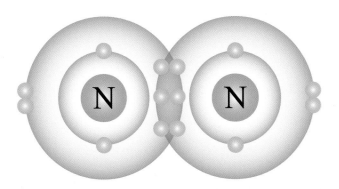

Sometimes, there can be three bonds connecting atoms in a molecule.

Ch-Ch-Ch-Changes

Molecules make up different kinds of matter. The types of atoms and their bonds give the matter its **properties**. This is the way things look and act.

Some properties are physical. The size of something is a physical property. Chemical properties have to do with how matter might change.

Physical properties can be seen or measured. They include color, size, and weight. Sometimes, physical properties change. A piece of paper may be ripped up. Still, its molecules stay the same.

A paper's white color is a physical property. Its ability to burn is chemical.

Chemical properties pave the way for chemical reactions. Some properties allow the bonds between atoms to break. Then, the atoms regroup in a new way. As they do, they form new molecules. The result has new physical and chemical properties.

Energy makes the atoms begin to move to start a reaction. While they are happening, some reactions let out energy. Others store it.

Heat is the most common form of energy that starts chemical reactions.

Parts of the Puzzle

Each chemical reaction has a couple of parts. At the start, there are **reactants** (ree-AK-tuhntz). Then, these things change. This leads to something new.

What comes out the other side? The things left at the end of a reaction are **products**. Their atoms are in different places.

Chemical reactions can be written as equations. Reactants are on the left. Products are on the right. In the middle, there is an arrow showing the change.

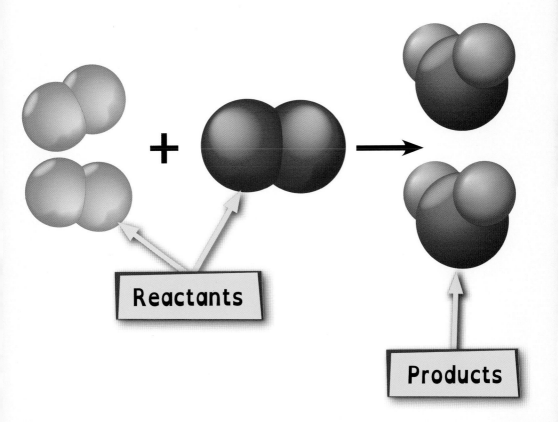

Reactants

Products

Finding the Balance

During chemical reactions, what changes and what stays the same? All changes are balanced. The amount of matter in reactants is equal to the amount in products. Matter isn't made or destroyed.

Matter may look different by the end of a chemical reaction. However, the reactants and products have the same number and types of atoms.

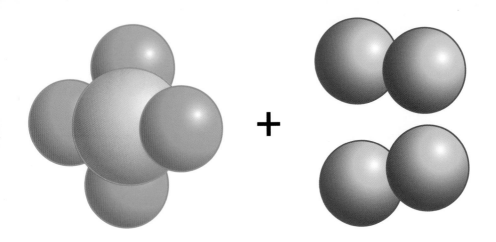

These reactants have nine atoms.

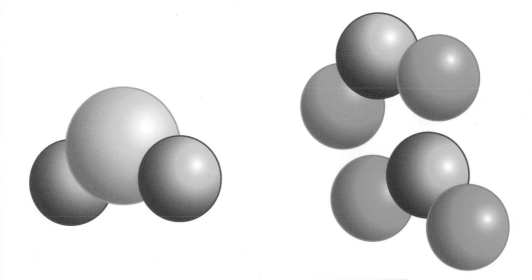

The same 9 atoms make up
the products of the reaction.

17

Building Up and Breaking Down

There are a few kinds of chemical reactions. A **synthesis** (SIN-thuh-sis) reaction is one where multiple reactants combine. They make a single new product. During **decomposition** (dee-kahm-puz-ZISH-uhn), a reactant is broken into two or more products.

Plants get food through another kind of chemical reaction. They start with carbon dioxide and water. Then, they take in energy from sunlight. The products are oxygen and sugar.

Photosynthesis is a chemical reaction.

In replacement reactions, atoms in the reactants switch spots. Then, there are new products.

Combustion (kuhm-BUS-chuhn), or burning, is a common chemical reaction. It takes some oxygen molecules to start. They interact with other molecules to form water and carbon dioxide. Often, this makes heat and light.

There are two kinds of replacement reactions. Sometimes, one bond between atoms is broken. A single new bond is formed. There may also be two bonds broken and formed.

Combustion often looks like a fire.

Fast and Slow

Different reactions happen at different speeds. Often, the more matter there is, the slower the reaction. High temperatures speed things along. More reactants can add speed, and fewer can slow things down. Chemical reactions can team up, too. One reaction may cause another to happen.

Explosions happen very quickly. These speedy chemical reactions may even set off more explosions. On the other hand, rusting takes time. It is a slow reaction.

You can add things to change the speed of a reaction. Something that speeds a reaction along is called a **catalyst** (KAT-uh-list). Want to slow a reaction? Add an **inhibitor** (in-HIB-i-tur). Some inhibitors can even completely stop a reaction.

Humans and other animals use catalysts and inhibitors every day. They are in our bodies. Catalysts help break down the food we eat.

We carry catalysts and inhibitors inside our bodies.

Reactions All Around

Chemical reactions are happening all the time. Sometimes, you can see the products of the reaction. Frying an egg causes a chemical reaction. Other times, it's less obvious. Your body breaking down the egg after you eat is a chemical reaction, too. Life wouldn't exist without chemical reactions.

Some chemical reactions end with products that are less tasty than a fried egg. Sour milk, moldy bread, and rotten fruit are all caused by chemical reactions.

Types of Chemical Reactions

Synthesis Reaction

A bond is formed.

A + B ⟶ A B

Decomposition Reaction

A bond is broken.

A B ⟶ A + B

Replacement Reaction

A bond is broken and a new bond is formed.
This can happen with one bond or two.

A B + C ⟶ A C + B

A B + C D ⟶ A C + B D

SilverTips for SUCCESS

★SilverTips for REVIEW

Review what you've learned. Use the text to help you.

Define key terms

catalyst

chemical bond

inhibitor

products

reactants

Check for understanding

Describe what a chemical property is and how it is related to a chemical change.

What are the parts that go into a chemical reaction called, and what is the name for what comes out of the reaction?

What can change the speed of a chemical reaction?

Think deeper

Why would someone want to be able to control the speed of a chemical reaction?

★SilverTips on TEST-TAKING

- **Make a study plan.** Ask your teacher what the test is going to cover. Then, set aside time to study a little bit every day.

- **Read all the questions carefully.** Be sure you know what is being asked.

- **Skip any questions** you don't know how to answer right away. Mark them and come back later if you have time.

Glossary

atoms the tiny building blocks that make up every substance in the universe

catalyst something that speeds up a chemical reaction

combustion a chemical reaction that produces heat and light

decomposition a chemical reaction where a reactant is broken into multiple products

inhibitor something that slows or stops a chemical reaction

molecules small things made from groups of atoms

products the things that are created by the end of a chemical reaction

properties the ways things look or act

reactants the things that exist before a chemical reaction starts

synthesis to combine two smaller or simpler things in a chemical reaction

Read More

Linde, Barbara M. *Makerspace Projects for Understanding Chemical Reactions (STEM Makerspace Projects).* New York: PowerKids Press, 2020.

O'Mara, Kennon. *Molecules (A Look at Chemistry).* New York: Gareth Stevens Publishing, 2019.

Rector, Rebecca Kraft. *Chemical Changes (Let's Learn about Matter).* New York: Enslow Publishing, 2020.

Learn More Online

1. Go to **www.factsurfer.com** or scan the QR code below.

2. Enter "**Chemical Reactions**" into the search box.

3. Click on the cover of this book to see a list of websites.

Index

About the Author

Daniel R. Faust is a freelance writer of fiction and nonfiction. He lives in Brooklyn, NY.